Baboo English As 'Tis Writ: Being Curiosities Of Indian Journalism

Arnold Wright

BABOO ENGLISH
AS 'TIS WRIT

Being Curiosities of Indian Journalism

BY

ARNOLD WRIGHT

London
T. FISHER UNWIN
PATERNOSTER SQUARE
MDCCCXCI

CONTENTS.

BABOO ENGLISH AS 'TIS WRIT.

CHAPTER I.

INTRODUCTORY SKETCH OF THE INDIAN PRESS.

THE Indian Press is in itself a curiosity. It is in some respects the oldest, in others the youngest, Press upon the face of the globe. Long before the *English Mercurie* was even dreamt of, every native Court in India had its *ukhbar*, or news-letter, giving the gossip of the Court, warlike and diplomatic as well as personal,

and in an extended way performing functions dis-
charged by the *Court Circular* in our own times.
Yet, despite this, it was not until three years after
the Battle of Waterloo had been fought and the
Times was well advanced on that career of use-
fulness which has made it the power it is in the
world, that India could boast of a printed native
newspaper of any kind, and it is well within our
own times that she possessed a print which did not
depend for its existence upon religious contro-
versies, a print which, in a word, was in the
modern sense a newspaper. As with its age so
in regard to its other features. Its polyglot character gives it a unique position amongst the
newspaper Press of the world. In about twenty
distinct languages it appeals to its readers. Side
by side with papers printed in the most irreproachable English—papers which would be no disgrace
to any town in England—are curious little broad-
sheets, no bigger than a pocket-handkerchief,
addressing their constituents through the medium
of a tongue the very name of which is unfamiliar
to European ears. Even Sanscrit—the Latin of

India—has its place amongst the newspapers, and the time is probably not far distant when the learned *pundits* of the East and the *savants* of the West will commune with each other in the pages of a print published in Zend or Pehlvi, or some other of the dead and half-forgotten languages of the remote past.

For all practical purposes the Press of India may, however, be divided into four distinct classes, *viz.*:—Anglo-Indian papers, native papers published in English, native papers published partly in English and partly in the vernacular, and native papers published entirely in the vernacular. Of the first of these classes it may be said that they bear favourable comparison with the Press of any part of the Empire outside the British islands. The principal organs are edited by men who have served an apprenticeship, and, in some cases, achieved distinction, on the English Press. Their list of contributors includes the most talented officials of the Indian Civil Service —the best educated bureaucracy in the world— and many of the articles they publish on special

subjects are worthy of a more lasting existence
than they secure in the ephemeral pages of a
newspaper. Their circulation, compared with
that of their English contemporaries, is exceedingly small, in no instance exceeding five thousand
daily ; but the number of their readers in proportion to their circulation is much larger, owing to
the heavy subscription necessarily charged. One
paper passes through many hands, and is read
and re-read before being finally consigned to the
waste-paper receptacle. Their readers are by no
means confined to the Anglo-Indian class. Educated natives read with avidity all that appears in
them, and nearly every Anglo-Indian paper has a
large number of natives amongst its regular subscribers. The proportion of native subscribers is
sometimes so large that the policy of the paper is
influenced in favour of native views. This is
especially the case in one or two instances where,
in addition to an extensive circle of native readers,
a paper has a partial or entire native proprietary.
In those cases the editorial policy is hardly, if in
any degree, to be distinguished from that of the

bonâ fide native papers. Questions are treated from the native standpoint, and special prominence is given to the points in the programme of the Indian political associations. The *Statesman* of Calcutta is the leading representative of this type of newspaper. It is owned by the Maharajah of Paikparra, a wealthy zemindar, or landowner, who takes a prominent part in horse-racing in India; and it was edited for many years by Mr. Robert Knight, a gentleman who had a remarkable career, and who for upwards of a quarter of a century was a conspicuous figure in the Indian political world. He went to India originally as a missionary nearly half a century ago, but deserted that calling in the first instance for mercantile pursuits, eventually, however, adopting a journalistic career. He was associated, at the outset, with the *Indian Statesman* and the *Times of India* at Bombay, in both of which journals he was a strong advocate of native views. Subsequently he proceeded to Calcutta and started there the *Statesman*, the paper which he edited to the time of his death, a year or two ago.

Mr. Knight was a type of a class of journalists once very numerous in India, but now rapidly dying out —men who, going out to India without even the elements of a journalistic training, took to Press work occasionally to obtain the means of livelihood, but more often than not in the first instance from sheer love of the work. These men, proceeding to their task without any of the traditions which curb the eccentricities or foibles of the average practised Press writer in this country, gave the Anglo-Indian newspapers an unconventionality of tone, which, to any one accustomed to the staid sobriety of home newspapers of the better class, was simply amazing. Personal matters, not necessarily scandalous or objectionable, were treated with a freedom which was oftentimes highly amusing. One instance in point, which will be readily called to mind by any resident of Bombay a couple of decades since, may be cited. It refers to an editor and manager—partners in one of the best newspapers in the country—who fell out, and carried on a singular duel in the columns of their own journal. The editor would indite a leader, dwelling upon the astonishing perversity and unmitigated impudence of his manager one day, and the manager would reply in the same column the next, assuring the editor that the feelings which animated him were entirely reciprocated. This kind of thing went on until the pair had either adjusted their differences or been told by their patrons that they had had quite enough of the squabble. Perhaps even a commoner form of eccentricity was for the editor to seize hold of some topic and present it in the leading columns in a startling form. One well-remembered instance of this kind was furnished somewhere in the forties by a paper called the *Mofussilite*, which was to the India of that day what the *Pioneer* is to ours. The great ecclesiastical dispute, Gorham *v.* the Bishop of Exeter, was at that time occupying men's minds and filling the columns of the newspapers at home ; and though it might have been a very absorbing topic to people in quiet country towns in England, it had but faint interest for Anglo-Indians. There was then no telegraph to India furnishing editors

with abundant matter for comment, and only a
monthly mail to keep India in touch with Europe.
Any curtailment of the supply of suitable news by
such a controversy was, therefore, rather a serious
matter ; and it was no easy thing to make a pre-
sentable appearance. The infliction was borne in
silence for some time, but when at length after
months had gone by, and the stream of dreary
disputation continued, the editor could bear it no
longer. He indited, perhaps, the shortest leader
that ever was written ; but that leader told the
whole story of his woes. It consisted only of
four words, and those words were, " Damn the
Gorham Case." The effect on the public was
wonderful. The paper sold like wild-fire, and
its circulation was permanently increased by at
least 20 per cent.

Such eccentricities as these are of the past
rather than the present, so far at least as the
leading journals are concerned, but there still
linger traces of the old spirit in quarters where
men of the old school still fill the editorial chair.
A book lent from the office library and not

returned, a missing address of some friend, or some matter of purely personal interest, are all considered of sufficient importance for an editorial note. Here, for example, is a paragraph which appeared in the principal Ceylon paper about the time of her Majesty's Jubilee : " The senior editor hopes no one will blame him *much*, if he indulges a little secret complacency in the reflection that in doing honour to the Queen in this her Jubilee year, all Ceylon will be unconsciously celebrating also *his* Jubilee year in the Island." For complacent egotism this would be hard to match anywhere, but scores of specimens of the same kind of personal writing might be given. The Anglo-Indian editor is a living personality, not a mere abstraction, and though he writes anonymously under cover of the editorial " we," his articles might frequently, by mere change of the pronoun, be transformed into a letter to which his signature was appended. " When we first came to India " ; " Illness has prevented us from noticing before," and similar phrases constantly appear in articles written by this stamp of editor.

But, as I have said, the race is dying out, and the chief Anglo-Indian papers are gradually losing their distinctive characteristics in the hands of the trained journalists into which they have now almost exclusively fallen.

Between the Anglo-Indian papers and the native papers of the better class there is not such a wide gulf as those unacquainted with India are apt to suppose. The native Press is young, but it is a vigorous product, and it has wisely followed on the lines of Anglo-Indian journalism in matters distinct from policy. The chief organs of native opinion—I speak now of those printed in English, such as the *Hindoo Patriot* of Calcutta, the *Indian Spectator* of Bombay, and the *Hindu* of Madras— are conducted in a scholarly manner and written in irreproachable English. Their editorial matter, when not disfigured by race prejudice or religious narrowness, might often be transferred bodily to their Anglo-Indian contemporaries without the difference being detected. There is, perhaps, a tendency to favour bombast and grandiloquence in treating of questions, but, on the whole, from a purely literary point of view, they afford little ground for criticism. This applies, however, to only a very few organs. The great majority are, it must be confessed, poor specimens of journalistic enterprise. Badly printed, badly written, and dragging on a miserable existence with a handful of subscribers who are always in arrears with their subscriptions, they are contemptible as organs of public opinion. They are for the most part edited by aspiring native students, whose imperfect knowledge of English leads them to perpetrate most ridiculous blunders. The injudicious use of metaphors and idioms is perhaps the greatest stumbling-block of the native writers. He has learned a number of expressions by rote, and is not content unless he is always dragging them into his writings whether the occasion warrants it or not. For example, one paper in referring to the death of a distinguished Englishman who had taken great interest in Indian affairs expressed a hope that the Almighty would "pour his mantle" on some other member of Parliament. Another journal in dealing with some

2

temporary disturbance of the political horizon in
Europe, thus commented on it : " We cannot
from a distance realize the intensity of the crisis,
but it is certain that *many crowned heads must be
trembling in their shoes.*" Again, during the excitement consequent upon the departure of Lord
Ripon from India, a writer in a Guzerati paper
suggested that a deputation of native princes and
gentlemen should "accompany his Excellency *and
see him safe home" ;* while the responsible head of
another journal expressed a hope that a certain
State might be saved from the ruin that " *threatens
it in the face.*" Ignorance of the dual meaning
attached to some words also, at times, produces
ludicrous results.   During the Franco-Chinese
War news came that the Shanghai Chamber of
Commerce had appealed to the British Government to prevent the blocking of the Woosung
bar by the Chinese—the bar of course being the
natural barrier at the mouth of the Woosung
river. A native editor entertaining strong views
of the oppressive character of British policy in
the East, immediately jumped to the conclusion

that a nefarious attempt was on foot against the liberties of the almond-eyed Celestial, and thus animadverted on the intelligence : " Woosung, we suppose is a Chinese town, and to prevent the overcrowding of the local Bar by Chinese lawyers is a monstrous proposal." " A monstrous meeting" is quite a common phrase with many native editors when they are anxious to accentuate the fact that a particular gathering was a very large one, and the " fatal loss " of steamers also enters into their vocabulary. In fact, there is scarcely an idiomatic or technical phrase in popular use which is not at some time or another misinterpreted and made to do strange service, to the amusement of the Anglo-Indian Philistine who reads the native papers.

The strictly vernacular Press is a sealed book to most Europeans. A few missionaries and officials there are who are capable of reading and understanding the contents of papers printed in one or two languages, but the great bulk of our countrymen in India are profoundly ignorant of the Press which appeals directly to the millions of India in their own tongue. Whatever knowledge we have of the vernacular Press is derived from official reports, the materials for which are furnished by native officials, and meagre translations in the columns of the Anglo-Indian Press also the work of natives. Little wonder is it, therefore, that the most divergent views should obtain as to the position, character, and influence of these papers, and their power for good or evil. The only point upon which most people are agreed is that these vernacular prints are disloyal and corrupt. That idea has been driven into the public mind by the publication from time to time of extracts of inflammatory articles directed against the Government, and by the arguments which have been adduced by the party in favour of their more stringent supervision. It would be useless to deny that there is not some justification for the view, but it is nevertheless open to serious doubt whether the vernacular Press has ever received full justice at our hands. We have been too apt to accept the ravings of one or two possibly obscure prints in one part of India as a fair specimen of the opinions of the united Press of the country, and to regard what is oftentimes a purely local malady for a disease which affects the whole system. There are no doubt organs of doubtful loyalty in every part of the country, but they find their most congenial home in Bengal, and it is from that quarter that nine-tenths of the elegant extracts upon which our opinion of the vernacular Press is based emanate. In Madras and Bombay the general tone of the indigenous Press is excellent. There are papers in those presidencies, like the *Bombay Samachar*, the *Rast Goftar*, and the *Kaiser-i-Hind* of Bombay, having a large circulation, which are capable of taking quite an Imperial view of public questions, and which are as free from suspicion of disloyalty as their Anglo-Indian contemporaries. Occasionally in periods of excitement, when race-hatreds are aroused by some passing event, they may give vent to intemperate language, but that is perhaps natural and even excusable under the circumstances. As a rule their attitude towards public questions is unexceptionable, and there is no more warrant for branding them as disloyal than there is in the case of the *Pall Mall Gazette,* or any other English organ which is outspoken in its language. A very good proof that the vernacular Press as a whole is not what it is popularly supposed to be in this country was furnished a few years ago during the discussion of the Penjdeh question. When the excitement consequent upon that incident was at its highest, and war was trembling in the balance, an important meeting of native editors was held at Madras, at which it was decided to refrain from all adverse criticism of the acts of Government until the danger which threatened should have passed away. To the credit of the native Press be it said, that during the whole period of the crisis the tone of the articles was beyond praise, and not a sentence was written which could give Russia the slightest reason to hope that she might count upon the support of the natives in the event of hostilities.

CHAPTER II.

EDITORIAL ANNOUNCEMENTS.

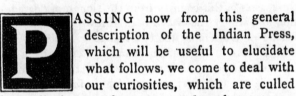ASSING now from this general description of the Indian Press, which will be useful to elucidate what follows, we come to deal with our curiosities, which are culled from all classes of papers, and embrace every department of the Press. Naturally in the order of things we begin at the very threshold of a newspaper's existence, and glance at the declarations with which the native editor embarks upon his career. They are almost invariably

written in pompous and inflated language, and
make a wonderful parade of patriotic virtue;
while the opportunity is never missed of pointing
out what a good work would be done by extending
the list of subscribers as much as possible. Here
is a sample taken from a bundle of similar an-
nouncements all couched in the same strain :—

" The object of the . . . may be stated short and
plain. It seeks to emancipate the people from the
fetters now forging for their feet ; to muzzle the en-
croachment of a devastating officialism ; to raise up
the masses of this country from the slough of degrada-
tion into which they have been thrown ; to fight the
battles of truth and liberty ; and to give life to the
new forces of the Indian people. Let each of its
friends become a missionary, carrying the light over
city and country, that we may find a future brighter
than even the present. Let any one man who desires
to help along the ' good time coming ' lead in his
neighbourhood, and thus scatter the acorns that may
grow into oaks."

There are, however, exceptions to these loud-

sounding addresses from new-fledged editors to
their readers. In their place are sometimes found
statements in which the subscribers are taken
into confidence in regard to difficulties which.
have troubled the good man at the head of
affairs in supplying "the long felt want."
Witness the following apology from an editor
of a new paper for the fact that a considerable
portion of one of its pages was left entirely
blank: "This is only the beginning of our
paper. We were not sure how much matter
was required to fill up our paper, and thinking
we had sufficient we did not exert ourselves to
get more. We, therefore, beg our readers will
excuse us this time for the space left blank, and
we hope to make ample amends in future." This
omission to fill certain columns is by no means
a rare instance of the kind. From another paper
we have the following notice : "Owing to an
unforeseen and unavoidable occurrence in our
establishment we were unable to fill the first
few columns of our paper with English matter
as usual. We, however, assure our readers that

we will be able to remove this difficulty and consequent inconvenience soon." More amusing even than either of these examples of struggling journalism is that furnished by yet another print which on the day of its birth came out with two blank pages, and in one of its columns boldly announced that some "specially interesting matter" had been held over "for want of space." An enlargement of a paper is always deemed sufficient justification for an "'address to readers." These are the pious terms in which a certain editor gloried in the fact that he had added to the number and length of his columns :—

"Our long cherished desire is at last realized. By the help of the great Almighty we now appear in broad size. We have succeeded to overcome the greatest of our numberless shortcomings, namely the shortness of our size. We have been working in the field of journalism for only six months and a half. Within this very limited space of time it has all along been our endeavour to merit public favour and patronage by adequate discharge of our legitimate duties

with undaunted and unbounded zeal and energy.
We launched ourselves on the field of cheap journalism in this country and with unabated perseverance
we have spared no pains and kept no stone unturned
to make the venture a perfect success. The present
development of this journal might be regarded by
many as the climax of success ; but we do not view
it in the same light, our ambition is not to be con-
tented so easily. We hope to make this journal, with
the help of Providence, still more improved and en-
larged." •

The default of subscribers is a continual source
of embarrassment to the Indian editor, and it is
upon this point that he probably feels most
strongly. One editor thus sarcastically addresses
his readers: "We beg to inform those subscribers upon whom we have lately called for
payment of their subscriptions, that editors and
newspaper servants do not live on stones, but
on diet almost similar to that which subscribers
feed on. We asked our stationers and the Post-
master-General to supply us with paper and
stamps respectively in exchange for seashells,

but they don't seem to see the economy of the
thing. We must, therefore, call upon our subscribers to pay up." Another writes in much
the same strain :—

" We took our birth in the year 1873 and continued
in the same condition till the end of the year 1882.
From the commencement of the present year we
increased our size by half, without any proportionate
increase of subscription. Some of our miserly subscribers grudge even to pay our dues. It is now
intended to again increase the bulk of the paper,
charging our subscribers the usual rate. Well, how
do you like the idea ? If we were to give a big sheet
instead of two or more pieces of paper, we should like
to know what effect it will produce ? We ask if the
operation of digesting the contents of a bigger sheet
would not cause dyspepsia to many of our readers ?
But pray send us our subscriptions in advance for the
ensuing year. Do not take into consideration the
interest chargeable on Re. 1-8 as advance subscription
for the year. An early payment of subscriptions will
prove encouraging."

It is not always that the backsliders are so

tenderly dealt with. There is a truculence about the following which one would think would scarcely be. calculated to produce results satisfactory to the newspaper's exchequer :—

" We have had a pretty good circulation all along, though not as much as we wanted. But our greatest trouble has arisen from dishonest subscribers, of whom it has been our misfortune to possess some, and whose default in payment has sadly crippled our poor resources. Having exhausted every possible means to rouse the attention and awaken the consciences of these gentlemen—having written them scores of letters from time to time without avail—and having at last even sent at considerable outlay a special messenger to them in the person of our Up-country Bill Collector, and still without any use ; we now as a last resort, our patience exhausted, have resolved upon the extreme step of gibbeting some of these precious gentlemen in a corner of our paper entitled ' Our Defaulting Subscribers,' and exposing to the world their real character and conduct for the use and edification of the simple-minded and unwary. It is with extreme reluctance and great pain we think of adopting this very disagreeable measure. But there is no help for it. It is only those who have defrauded us of our just dues who will figure so unenviably before the world. We hope this warning will induce one and all bad paymasters among our subscribers to pay up."

This is also written in a style which betrays a considerable amount of irritation on the part of the presiding genius, combined with a loyal fervour which is truly commendable :—

" Among the Native Government officials who are subscribers to this paper, an idea prevails that as such they, have a right to get almost everything under the sun without payment. What will our readers say when we tell them, that one of these officials who unsolicited asked the manager of this paper to send it to his address and after perusing it week after week for two years at last persistently refused to pay its subscriptions. . . . Up to this hour we have received no encouragement from those of our citizens who are known as educated Hindus. In spite of all these discouragements we shall press forward and onward, leaving the result in the hands of that Being who knows our difficulties and trials. We have to-day christened the *Herald*, The *Jubilee* and we cannot but invoke the spirit of the living God to bless our Queen-Empress Mother with all His choicest blessings. May she live long to reign over us. May Her reign be as prosperous as it has been in the past. May war and rumours of war cease. May the world recognize in Her the brightest example of all that is good and worthy of imitation?"

Addresses on the New Year, without which no native newspaper is considered complete, are also productive of curious reflections. Piety, politics, and pecuniary and personal matters, are about equally blended; occasionally with startling results. Take for an example the following :—

"One more year has rolled on in the boundless expanse of time. One more span has run on in the great circle of eternity. Another twelvemonth *of our destined end* has passed away. A new year has set in, and with it a new era of our life has begun. With the advent of the new year the —— enters the second year of its existence."

This is also very pretty :—

"The year 1885 has departed. Yesterday as we awoke in the morning, we stood face to face with the New Year, which, with a cheerful countenance, thus addressed us :—'Behold, I am come and brought with me for you new works and new duties, and also new honours and new triumphs. I have opened for you a new field of action. I expect that with new hopes, a new vigour and a new determination, you will enter the arena, finish those works of which the dead year has not seen the completion, and accomplish as much of the new works, as will crop up around you during the short period of my sojourn.'

"The year 1886 has launched us into the second year of our existence. We thank God that, by his assistance, we have been able to discharge faithfully the duties which we had volunteered to perform, and we hope, with greater Divine assistance and larger support from our co-religionists, for whose service we have girt up our loins, we will be able to enlarge the sphere of our actions.

"Not knowing what the Future has in store for us, and not having the power to peer into its secrets, the wisest course, at the close of a year, is to look behind and see how much ground we have traversed in 'Life's awful journey,' and how much work entrusted to us has been performed and how much left undone, that we may understand how much effort we must put forth to bring them to completion."

CHAPTER III.

FREE-AND-EASY JOURNALISM.

ATIVE Indian Journalism is conducted on free-and-easy principles.
An editor thinks nothing of sus-
pending the issue of his paper for
what in England would be regarded
as the most trivial reasons, and when he deems it
necessary to apologize for the omission he usually
does so in the airiest fashion. Here is a specimen
of the customary style of amend :—

"The vast circulation of the —— has necessitated

considerable augmentation of our Establishment, and we have, therefore, been obliged to remove our Printing Works and Office to a more commodious premises.

" These arrangements prevented the issue of the —— last week, but we hope and trust our readers will kindly overlook it, as it was unavoidable.

" The only alternative left was to have the number printed in Calcutta, but the vast circulation of the —— presented an insuperable difficulty, and no Printing Firm in Calcutta was prepared to undertake the job either for love or for money.

" We promise, however, to make a handsome reparation for this loss to our subscribers—and that before the Xmas tide."

This same editor, on being remonstrated with by an indignant subscriber for his frequent failures to keep his engagements, coolly remarked that the paper had not appeared as he was anxious " to take time to refresh his vigour."

The following is more subdued in tone :—

" We are very sorry that owing to an accident the

last two issues of this paper did not come out till now. We are at the same time glad to tell our subscribers that we have, after all, *secured a Press of our own ; and we* shall soon get rid of the disadvantages we were hitherto under, in getting the *Herald* printed in other Presses. As we have to remove the Press to its proper locality and to settle down every arrangement connected with it, we ask our Subscribers to grant us leave till the 12th of June, after which date the work will be resumed and every regularity will be observed in the issue and despatch of the paper in time. We would not have asked for this concession, had the financial condition of this office been quite satisfactory ; our financial condition would have been quite satisfactory, had all of our subscribers been regular in paying attention to their part of the business. We would, however, urge upon them to observe that it is a high time now, when they should come forward to give us their helping hand, if not with large advances, at least with clearing up the balance due already and the subscription up to the end of the current quarter."

The poor editor's troubles were not, as he confidently anticipated, surmounted when he had obtained a press of his own. The paper failed to

appear the following week, and when at length it
burst once more upon an expectant world, the
notice given above was reproduced with this
" explanation " :—

" With reference to the above Notice we beg to
state that, as while arranging to remove in hurry our
newly purchased Press many of the type cases fell *in
pie*, we are obliged to take more time than we otherwise expected to do in resuming the work.   Moreover
the news is also dull in these days.

" Under the above circumstances we ask to be
allowed time till the end of this month to complete
our arrangements satisfactorily.   Should any important
news be received during this time, we shall bring it
to the information of our subscribers by issuing an
Extra.

" If any of our subscribers be particular about their
subscription, we shall even undergo one month's price
of this paper for its suspension during june instant."

Occasionally causes quite outside the limits of
the newspaper office are sought to excuse delay in
the despatch of a paper to its subscribers.   The
following is from a journal published at Goa, in

Portuguese-India, and is, therefore, as likely as not to have been justified by facts : " Owing to the absolute want of postage stamps in the Government Post Office we regret having been obliged to detain the two preceding issues of this paper which are now forwarded to our subscribers."

It is, however, to holidays and festivals that most of the temporary disappearances of papers are due. The editor takes his relaxation with the rest of the crowd, and gives himself leave in the most matter-of-fact way. One of the fraternity thus writes :—

"With the consent of our readers we propose taking our annual holiday of a fortnight. The whole country now enjoys respite from labour, and we are sure our readers will not begrudge us our annual holiday during this season of rest and relaxation."

Another condescends to be apologetic :—

"Our constituents will, we hope, excuse us for taking what may be called French leave on the last

Thursday. The Sancrat Holiday ranks with us, more than any other Holiday. In our issue of the 6th Instant we ought to have given notice to the effect that we intended to take a Holiday on the 13th Instant. We fail to do so and this was due to the fact that we learnt too late that the Sancrat Holiday fell on our paper-day. We ask our sympathisers and supporters to excuse us. We have stated above the true cause of our absence on the last Thursday, and we doubt not that we shall be excused by our supporters."

But the gem of our collection of *apologia* is the following brief but pregnant announcement: "Our next paper day falling on Christmas Day, *the next issue of this journal will not appear.*"

It frequently happens that others beside native papers are affected by holidays. Witness the following from an English paper published in a great centre of Mahommedan activity :—

"Owing to the *Dasehra* and *Mohurrum* celebrations —emphasized by the fact that our establishment is wholly a native one and likely to be materially

demoralized through their religious proclivities and
general zeal for turning the week into a thorough-
going carnival season,—it is very likely we shall have
to ask the indulgence of our readers in the matter of
some reduction in the pages of the next two numbers
of the ——. We shall not presume upon our subscribers' kindness, however, to a greater extent than is
absolutely unavoidable."

Here is another announcement of the same
class :—

" Owing to the recurrence of the annual celebration
of the *Bakhra Eed* by the Muhammadan community
yesterday,—added to the circumstance that our working staff is in the main composed of members of that
religious sect—we were under the necessity of going
to press the best way we could with our present number ; being so short-handed, indeed, that we have
been compelled to leave over much local, editorial, and
other matter, for the simple reason that the staff were
not prepared to make a sacrifice of prospective spiritual
blessings in order to avoid a full measure of managerial
maledictions. We can only, on the present occasion,
apologise to our readers for all shortcomings. It is

not our fault, but is distinctly due to an excess of religious zeal on the part of our *employés*, who not only bid defiance to editorial fulminations—but even laugh to scorn Jove's mighty thunderings with the greatest nonchalance possible."

A third extract we have at hand shows that loyalty as well as religious devotion is responsible occasionally for laxity in Indian newspaper offices :—

"We must ask the indulgence of our readers this week for any shortcomings that may be found in this issue—the fact is our compositors yield in loyalty to none, and we have been obliged to grant them three days' leave in honour of her Majesty's jubilee."

It also frequently happens that sickness on the editorial staff, probably composed of a man and a boy, or it may be of a single unit, deprives a paper of its most conspicuous feature. This is the sort of intimation often met with : " Owing to illness among our editorial staff our leading columns are a blank this evening."

Sometimes a reason less creditable than mere indisposition is availed of to excuse deficiencies. One editor thus introduces his New Year's paper to his readers :—

"We are sorry to find our collaborateurs have not yet recovered from the effects of the enjoyments of the holidays which have just passed away. Our post-bag has been very poor during the last few days, and beyond our usual exchanges nothing original has been received. The past two weeks have been those of mirth and enjoyment in every part of the civilized world, and we trust our readers and subscribers will overlook the rather dry appearance of the —— this week."

Another editor—a native Christian—anxious to announce the rumoured demise of a local official of standing to his readers during the Christmas week found himself confronted with an insuperable obstacle :—

"We received," he says, "several *chits* (*Anglice*, letters) each informing us that a certain person had shuffled off his mortal coil, and this rumour appeared

to be true because the party named left —— in a
critical state of health. We immediately despatched
a messenger to get one or two of our 'devils' to publish an extra, but there was not a single sober fellow
available."

The relations between editors and their corres-
pondents are of a peculiar kind, and the former
think nothing of gibbeting the latter in the
columns of their paper. " If you cannot give us
more interesting news we must part," is the curt
note appended to the certainly feeble lucubrations
of one of the local contributors. " Your communication is written in such shabby English that
we cannot give it insertion." " Not at all interesting. We will hold your communications over
until we require padding; at present we have
interesting matter to fill our columns with," are
intimations given to other literary aspirants, while
another is still more bluntly told: " Your cali-
graphy shows that you were under the influence
of Bacchus when you wrote your epistle—for we
have not seen such specimens of handwriting in our

lives. Try and write more legibly when you next
write to us." Finally "Our Sleepy Corres-
pondents" are addressed in these terms: "We
have not heard from many of our contributors this
week, and must rouse them from their lethargy.
Are their pens silenced by the approach of
Christmas?"

CHAPTER IV.

NATIVE QUACK ADVERTISEMENTS AND OBITUARY NOTICES.

EAVING these specimens of editorial eccentricity we come now to deal with what concerns the advertising and news columns of a native newspaper. For the most part editors very wisely take their matter bodily from the Anglo-Indian papers, even the advertisements—many of which are probably of a bogus description inserted to give an air of prosperity to the concern. Several columns are, however, set apart for original contributions, and the delver in these finds a mine of curious material. Taking the advertisements first it may be noted that the native quacks furnish the greatest proportion of our collectanea. Many of them are much too free in their language to be reproduced here at all, while all require judicious editing. The publication of testimonials testifying to the virtues of a particular medicine is the commonest form of advertisement. Here is one, a fair sample of many of the same kind : " This is to cartify Mr. Joowaladutt Debidut he got purgative pills, very good ; I recommend to take any one ; I used many times that pills." Frequently also the native *hakim* or doctor seeks the favours of the public through the medium of a loud-sounding proclamation, in which he vaunts his skill in extirpating every disease that flesh is heir to, and many others that the majority of mankind wot not of. Here is one which appeared in the original surmounted with the Royal Arms :—

"I the undersigned obedient monk and Tomb's

slave of Khaja Mainudin Chishti emperor of India inhabitant of Ajmere most humbly beg to every one gentleman, that if anybody might be suffering with demon, fairy, magic and fury, from any long time, or if any woman is barren, offspring is dying, or any sort of patient, who cannot be cure by any sort of medical treatment, they should attend at Mote Bazar in Memon Kader Fakir Mohomed's house No. 383 from 6 to 12 a.m. and 3 to 5 p.m. all the above-mentioned patients will be cure by pronouncing some words and blowing upon water, spiting and amulet, by the grace of Almighty Creator.

" If anybody is suffering with weakness and privacy in eyes, they will be cure by the medicine.

" If any body wishes to take examination for the above mentioned questions, the undersigned can answer for his any question very easily and several times the undersigned was made contrast with great enchanter in Calcutta at Kalighat and in Malbar, but by the grace of God Khaja saket the under-signed has been successful upon them.

" Some days ago the undersigned was in Calcutta for many days, and he cured there lots of patients by the grace of God, which was related by the Calcutta News-papers, hoping several gentlemen might be known by reading the Calcutta newspapers, and the late Governor General Lord Ripon were very kind on the undersigned on account of above mentioned abilities, and many times I had been visited with them in Calcutta and Shamla, and surely nobody will return hopeless from the door of Khaja Mainudin Chishti emperor of India by the grace of God.

"The above mentioned time from 6 to 12 p.m. is appointed for treatment and from 3 to 5 for communication."

The following is brief and to the point :—

" By the grace of Almighty Creator I can cure any disease whatever without medicine and acceptance of any fee. The external disease can be cured within few minutes, and internal ones of course require one day per year. This has been acquired for me through the kindness of a Faquer. I have cured 300 persons at Khiljeepore, C.I., 300 at Rajgorh, C.I., 1,000 at Beora, C.I., 200 at Suthaha, C.I., and 200 at Nuxoodangosh, C.I."

This is also amusing :—

" Notice is hereby given that this Medical Court is

advantageous to every patient suffering from Feet swelling, who can be cured by my Medical treatment. Any man belonging to this or any out country, suffering from Magic or devils, and that cannot be cured by English or Native Doctors, is sure to be cured by my treatment. A devil causes woman's offspring obstruct its growth will be set at liberty without giving trouble. Poors can get medicine in Charity. Captious and mischievous will not be allowed in my dispensary, and such patients can never be cured. Any man quite acquainted in every kind of Magic should try his skill on me. Any disease that cannot be cured by any English or Native Doctors, will be cured by me in uttering a word only.

"Any one wishing to try his skills with mine should do it in a private place. Poors can get medicine from 7 a.m. to 9 a.m., and rich from 9 a.m. to 12 p.m. Jokers or mischievous will certainly be given in charge of Police. Asthma and Cough will be cured by me and Empress of India shall receive the blessings of such cured Patients.

"May God bless Empress of India and prolong her life, and prosper her in the present and next world."

For poetry of language, combined with assurance, this would be hard to beat :—

4

"Notice.—Come pensive, go in ease. Light being the fresh flower in garden of life, and eye a light for dark abode of family. I am encouraged by my sanguine anxiety to record with my unfeigned joy, the competency of a occulist which, I have valiently performed most effective and interesting one to the residents of Mecca, Judda, and other places. Vide certificates on view, and thereby draw attention of those patients suffering from blind eyes, and to my curator house, No. ——, situate at ——, with a view to promptly obtain cure with great ease and short time, to cherish the lustre of eye-sight. Visiting hours from 7 a.m. to 6 p.m. for opinion advanceable, if it is worth operating and treating with. For the poor gratis in the name of heaven to exalt my operation cherishable garihire chargeable when invited at home for examination and Council if curable, with a view to relieve Patients from pain of extending consciousness. —Shekh Bahadar, Hakim."

From native doctors' puffs to obituary notices is, perhaps, not a great stride, for if the quack does not succeed in killing his patient it is not for want of trying. In these *post mortem* references the Indian writer is seen in his most ambitious

mood. His flights of eloquence are sometimes
positively startling in their airy splendour. He
loves to court the sublime, and in the process as
often as not drops upon the ridiculous. Most of
the writings of this class have to be read in their
entirety to be adequately appreciated, but the
following closing passage of a notice of the death
of a certain native prince may be quoted :—

" Dear Mr. Editor, where in the world can a prince
of his merits, a prince in whom meet the rare com-
bination of such noble qualities be found ? But alas !
what is the good of my saying all these now ? He is
already ' a saint in saint with Heaven.' My eyes
dear Editor while I write this are so full of tears that
I scarcely see the motion of my pen, and therefore
excuse me if I conclude this rather abruptly. I am
out of myself with sorrow. It is true that death is
inevitable and that we are like so many bubbles on the
ocean. I can understand also what Shakespeare means
by saying ' 'tis but the time, And drawing days out
that men stand upon.' But all these philosophical
reflections do not in the least seem to diminish the
sorrow which weighs heavily upon my heart. On the
other hand they only tend, I know not why, to

accelerate the copious flow of tears trickling down my cheeks. May His Highness meet with a cordial reception in the celestial world, as he has every where met with while in this terrestrial world of ours. With this I conclude."

It will be noticed that the writer of the above closes his communication with a pious wish for the happiness of the deceased prince in the next world. This is a characteristic common to nearly all these effusions. " May his soul rest in peace in heaven ! " " May the Almighty take him unto Himself ! " and " It pleased God to snatch away from us one of our great benefactors, and we must all submit to His will," are expressions which are frequently met with in papers, whose devotion to the Hindoo or Mahommedan faith is beyond suspicion. In fact, the most devout organs of Methodism or Congregationalism are not more copiously interlarded with pious reflections than the native papers on these occasions. There is no reason to doubt the sincerity of the writers, but it is probable that they have borrowed their modes of expression from missionary literature, with which they are most of them well acquainted.

CHAPTER V.

THE NATIVE DESCRIPTIVE REPORTER.

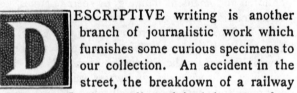ESCRIPTIVE writing is another branch of journalistic work which furnishes some curious specimens to our collection. An accident in the street, the breakdown of a railway train, or a flood, are all exploited in turn; but, above all things, the native reporter, like the English penny-a-liner, is most at home at a fire. We have in the following a characteristic specimen of this sort of writing:—

"I solicit the favour of your kindness to assign a

corner in your renowned paper to the following horri-
pilating accident of fire-break at Jamalpur on the 31st
ultimo.

"When the clock struck about one on day a fire
broke out in Naogong (Boidyapara), the eastern
quarter of Jamalpur. The wind was high, and about
an hour was sufficient to show the hideous aspect of
horrid fire. Minutes take time to tell them, but the
rage of fire takes not ten minutes to run from house
to house and to hop on a sudden over hundreds of
huts.

"Females with sucking babes embracing them, and
children and maidens hanging by their relatives, with
heart-rending wailings and outcries, ran out to the
road, and to seek shelter confusedly ran away, some
towards the hill about a mile off, some to the bunga-
lows inhabited by the Europeans here. To add to the
calamity wells were dry, and water was rare. Shocking news then spread out on all sides. Clerks from all
offices were freely allowed to run out to the burning
spot and exerted their mustard force to abate the rage
of blazing fire. But the Europeans deserve commendable mention of their philanthropic deeds and heroic
achievements.

"Mr. Campbell the Loco Superintendent stood for-

ward with his stalwart frame in front of the horrid
fire, and his commanding tone of angelic voice, mingled
with his own example, to save the properties and the
lives of the poor creatures, inspired awe, respect and
veneration to the silent by-standers, and drew them up
like Roman phalanx to assist him in the deeds. But
this was not all. He ordered his shop-coolies to hasten
to the wells and in want of water, then to the only
tank, about a quarter mile distant, and in an instant
water was on hand's end. Messrs. Hartley, Nixon,
Dixon, and the Rev. Dowding, with their lives at frequent stake, stood on the burning huts amid constant
boomings and loosened away the blazing roofs with
mighty strength and Herculean labour that astound the
natives to behold from afar. They were also simul-
taneously busy to pump water to the tops of houses
with extraordinary agility and bravity that make our
hair stand on end, and our senses on their standstill.
Similar were the friendly deeds of many more
Europeans, whose names to tell would engross a long
sheet of paper. Mr. Campbell has done more. He
gives shelter to the houseless vagrants, and assists
them in every possible way.

"The silver tides of truly philanthropic feelings
that gush forth from the pure fountain of their souls

cannot but claim our dump praise, as words are insufficient to give forms and shapes to their magnanimous
character and noble feelings."

The following graphic account of a fire on board
a ship by a native reporter is also interesting :—

"The S.S. *Clan Rannoch*, which arrived in the
Bombay harbour yester morn, from London, with a
miscellaneous Cargo on board, was discovered on
Thursday last to be on fire while at sea. Her master
is Captain Stuart R. Lee, a short, carroty-whiskered,
intelligent, wiry officer. She hoisted the flag of
danger on anchoring near the Mazagon Dock, and was
on that account promptly visited by the marine and
port officers. The origin of the fire for the present
remains buried in mystery. The Captain himself
knows not, the Port Officer Captain Morland little, the
Superintendent of the water division police the least,
the officer of H.M.'s Customs and Excises nothing.
"From five in the morning up to a late hour in the
evening the human humming and busy bustle was one
continuous scene on board. It had calms at intervals
no doubt. The extent of the fire, which had burnt
and destroyed for five consecutive days, notwithstand-

ing all the devoted efforts of an excellent captain and
his crew to control it, must have been enormous.
Although no belching forth of flames could be descried
yesterday, the constant emission of hot steamy smoke
was enough to convince the most sceptical observer
that the road to ruin was being surely and steadily
followed.

"The pumps that were going on from eight in the
morning were allowed a short respite at 3 p.m. It
was just to see what good they had done. After a few
minutes' interval they were again under requisition.
It vexed warm at four. Redoubled exertions were
made with renewed vigour by the already exhausted
men. Davies vociferated his instructions to the
Lascars on the top of his lungs, the chief engineer on
board, Mr. Macfarlane, gruffly orders his subordinates
to look to the constant supply of steam power for the
proper working of the pumps. Whether the captain
descries danger or what, but instantly he drops under
the hold, bluffly cheers his men on. It was all bustle
and confusion at the time on the after-hold of course,
the working of the pumps on their full power speed
making the confusion worse confounded. Box after
box, bale after bale, package after package, are either
hoisted by steam cranes or thrown alongside by manual

labour. Heavy lumber boats of landing agents and
the customs were in readiness to receive the motley
goods. Seething vapours, as if issuing from a boiling
cauldron, and steamy smoke, as if emitted from the
burning mouth of a horrible dragon, come forth in
tremendous, nauseating, sickening volumes. The
efforts are slackened, either they are of no avail or
they are not wanted. Out comes the captain first, the
men follow him on the deck, the pump on board stops,
but the water barge keeps up its howling noise, inter-
mingled with a deafening din. Parties of three and
four stand consulting ; there is a calm, everything
seems to be at a standstill. The smoke and vapours
subside, but the hoses keep on pouring water, for the
clue to the locality is considered to be found out,
therefore the calm must have followed the volumes.

"It seems to have been decided to direct all the
united efforts to lighten the after-hold under water by
taking out as much of the goods as lay within reach.
To that end all people work. From the upper layers
some tons weight was removed. Fifty tons will be the
maximum lifted, says the dubash. To clear the contents of all the holds, main, fore, and aft, will take
eight days, says the same Parsee.

"The captain looks thoughtful, his forehead is

marked with wrinkles of care and grief. Even the
redoubtable Davies can bear no longer, out leaps he
with a long jump ; after a while down he goes back,
his long cloth *camise* (shirt) and breeches are all
bespattered with water and coal dust ; he sees, he
surveys, he pokes his head between the still hot boxes
in the hold to ascertain the locality of the fire. His
silken kerchief tied round his ample forehead in the
Parsi lady fashion bore a strange head-dress in comparison with his burly strong stature and healthy
ruddy constitution. He looks tired, he sits down at
haphazard on a chance seat. Comes he up the bridge,
lies down at full stretch on the planks with the face
and belly in close contiguity with the flooring. He,
the first man who went underneath the hatch without
fear or fail, who shrank not for a moment from struggling with the strong flame-like smoke that was being
belched forth manfully and sturdily for five mortal
hours, can no longer bear the indolence of repose,
when he hears busy voices all around him, so up he
starts, descends the bridge ladder again, and silently
assists at the emptying of the cargo. Now everything
seems to be common cooly work, such as is not
unusually seen when a boiler is being shifted from the
dockyard to a spinning and weaving mill.

"The cargo, consisting of biscuit boxes, paper reams, pale ales, also contain some combustibles and explosives, such as spirits, brandies, paint, oils. If that would have taken fire a terrible result would have been the consequence. But the united efforts of the port and marine officers present saved the steamer. At least the safety was regarded as ensured at 7 p.m., when the fire was smouldering."

Before quitting this branch of the subject we cannot refrain from quoting two further samples of native reporting, both of which are amusing, though in different ways. The first is an account of an accident at a mill, accompanied by some suggestions of a practical character, which show the writer in the light of a reformer :—

"On last Sunday, at about 4.30 p.m., the Nagpur world round about the Empress Mills was startled by a shocking accident. A young boy aged 14 years, while working at the throstle in the said mills, was caught by the end of his *dhotee* (loin cloth), and then in a few seconds gave up his ghost, his skull being all fractured. These flaunting *dhotees* have proved the bane of so many young innocent lives, that in these days of general improvement and precaution, it seems very inconsistent why cannot any means and precautionary measures be devised, in the shape of a "mill-dress," which will curtail the mortality thus caused yearly. I would just suggest that a short breeches coming up to the knees, quite body-tight, and a jacket on the same principle would in a great degree prevent such shocking accidents."

The second affords an example of native wit at the expense of the ruling race :—

"A British-born seaman, with the appropriate name of Butcher belonging to the B. S. *Nebo*, last Saturday evening in Bowbazar Street, made a sport of an elderly native by striking him on the head. The effect of the joke was instantaneous. The poor Indian fell down insensible and died in Hospital."

CHAPTER VI.

NATIVE HUMOUR AND POETRY.

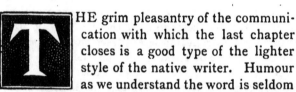

HE grim pleasantry of the communication with which the last chapter
closes is a good type of the lighter
style of the native writer. Humour
as we understand the word is seldom
if ever met with in the native Press. There are
no columns of witty sayings or jokes such as are
common to most English papers, and on the rare
occasions that the Indian writer does condescend
to be frivolous, there is invariably a political
object underlying his humour. A favourite device
of the native wit is to take some well-known

English production and parody it. Thus during
the height of the acrimonious controversy over
the Ilbert Bill, when some hot-headed Anglo
Indians in Calcutta were talking of opposing the
measure by force of arms, if carried; Hamlet's
soliloquy was presented in the following guise :—

" To rise, or not to rise,—that is the question :—
Whether 'tis manlier in the White to suffer
The ills of Ilbert's Jurisdiction Bill,
Or to take arms against Old England's rule,
And, by opposing, end it ?—To arm,—to fight ;—
No more ; and, by sheer force, to say we end
The heart-ache, and the fear of equal law
Of British Zubberdusts.(oppressors), why, 'tis an end
Devoutly to be wish'd. To arm,—to fight ;—
To fight ! perchance to bolt :—ay, there's the rub ;
For in that flight for life what ills may come,
When we have shuffled off our Sovereign's yoke,
Must give us pause : there's the respect
That makes a long howl of an exile's life ;
For who would bear the scorns of Ripon's rule,
The Moslem's wrong, the Hindu's contumely,
The pangs of despised pride, the law's restraints,
The insolence of Babus, and the spurns

That free-born Britons of the Government take,
When he might save himself from thraldom vile
With Volunteers' arms ? Who would not unfurl
Rebellion's red flag on Fort William's heights
But that the dread of failure in the field,—
Of transportation home, home from whose wants
We hither all have fled,—puzzles the will,
And makes us rather bear this Ilbert Bill,
Than fly to other ills we know not of ?
Thus fear makes simple braggarts of us all ;
And thus the *British* hue of resolution
Is blackened o'er with *nigger* cast of thought ;
And Anglo-Indian schemes of independence,
With this regard, become mere sound and fury
And lose the name of action."—

A more daring writer about the same time came
out with the subjoined parody of the opening
chapters of Genesis :—

" BOOK OF GENESIS.

CHAPTER I.

In the beginning Jove created England and India.
The former was called the Heaven and the latter
Earth.

(2) And great was the misrule and anarchy that prevailed on earth. And darkness brooded upon it. And the spirit of Anglo-Indian selfishness moved upon its surface.

(3) And Jove filled the Heaven with Whites and the earth with black niggars.

(4) And Jove blessed the Whites and said unto them, 'Be fruitful and multiply, and replenish the earth also, and subdue it ; and have dominion over the black niggars of earth, and over the fowls of the air and over every living thing that moveth upon the earth.'

(5) And Jove said unto the black niggars also— 'Behold, I have placed Thee under the dominion of the Whites. Therefore, be not so rash and inconsiderate as to aspire after the rights and privileges enjoyed by those white people.'

(6) And Jove saw everything that he made, and behold, it was very good.

CHAPTER II.

These are the generations of heaven and of the earth when they were created.

(2) But the earth was without light. And Jove

5

said, let the earth be enlightened by Western Education and so there sprung up a race of Keranees with torches to dispel the darkness.

(3) But behold! along with this Western Education there cometh light.

(4) And for sometimes this light was supposed to be good. For it was very good.

(5) But behold the light soon began to dazzle the sight of the Anglo-Indian selfishness. And they tried to extinguish this light. But it was too powerful to be extinguished.

(6) And by this light, the black niggars of the earth felt that they were naked.

(7) And for sometimes they were not ashamed of it.

CHAPTER III.

Now, the serpent of the Western Education was more subtile than any beast of the field which Jove had made.

(2) And this serpent said unto the black niggars— 'Yea, hath Jove said ye shall never aspire to become equal to the Whites.'

(3) And black niggars said into this serpent,—

'Yes, Jove hath said unto us that—ye shall not aspire to become equal to the Whites, but you die.'

(4) And the serpent said unto the black niggars—'Ye shall not surely die. For Jove doeth know that in the day ye aspire after an equality with the Whites your eyes shall be opened, and ye shall be as whites, knowing good and evil.'

(5) And when the black niggars saw that it was good to aspire after the rights and privileges of the Whites, they did aspire after them.

(6) And the eyes of these niggars were opened. And they became vociferously clamorous.

(7) And Jove hastened to the earth, and they heard the voice of Jove walking before them.

(8) And the black niggars hid themselves from the presence of Jove amidst the trees.

(9) And Jove called unto the black niggars and said unto them, where art thou?

(10) And the black niggars said unto Jove, 'We heard Thy voice but we were afraid of you lest you send us to Hareen Baria Jail[1] for contempt of Court, because we were naked, and so we hid ourselves.'"

Occasionally also official documents are simi-

[1] The principal Calcutta jail.

larly turned to ridicule, but a check was put to
the practice not long since by the Government,
who found that spurious versions of confidential
papers were being presented in such a form as to
lead the reader to think they were genuine.

Poetry is another ally upon whom the Indian
political writer is accustomed to rely. The lines
are invariably the most contemptible doggerel,
but there is no mistaking the sentiments. Take
the following as an example :—

> " We are neither Protestan's
> Catholics, Presbetrians,
> Time and History earthen,
> Vedas' followers, black heathen.
> Lesser number Moslems are,
> They too, ask us in despair :—
> ' Why are money spent on Churches ?
> Chaplains, priests, Bishops, Arch's ? '
> Colleges and schools of Sanskrit,
> Nemnuks old——of Shastree, Pandit,
> Dakshinas of Veidic Bhut,
> Almost all to-day are shut.
> Spend enormous sums on *Church*,

Mission schools, the way is such !
Why our money spent on churches,
Mission grants and Bishops, Arch's ?

Germans !   See their ardent zeal,
Learning Sanskrit, they reveal
Ancient stock of Indian knowledge,
Number of their School and College.
Is increasing for our Sanskrit
Thanks to them, with highest credit.
Under England's noble rules
Brahmins getting drunk and fools !
Shastrees, Veidics, dying fast,
Ancient knowledge dead at last.
Sanskrit old, why not promoted ?
Why on Churches money wasted ?

Parel wanted Christian Church,
Christians for endowments search.
Sir Fergusson eulogised,
Narrow heart was magnimised.
Seven hundred pounds he offers
From Hindustan's sinking coffers.
Seven thousand rupees *said*,
Sixteen thousand *have been paid !*
Hindus, Moslems *will* complain,

Hearing complaints *we* refrain.
All must pay for Christian Churches,
Chaplains, Priests, Bishops, Arch's !

Now we hear from Allahabad,
New Bishópric they have had !
Indian money this way spent
Causes people discontent.
In the sight of God and man,
None would like this ugly plan.
Question raised for years forty,
Opinions have variety.
Do not concur in the views,
Calmly wasting immense dues.
Lord Kimberley plainly said :—
' Serious complaints are not made !
Parl'ment cares not Indian cry
Things in silence often die !
Twenty-two lacs yearly haunted
For these Churches !—Justice wanted."

Still more pointed is the meaning of these lines,
which were addressed to a high official, who
undertook a sweeping reduction of the establishment of a certain Government department :—

"To Mr. ———, C.S.

"You are not the man of high-minded,
Going to harm the men who are depended.
You are not fit for the post, being unkinded man,
You will be soon stabbed like Mr. Norman.
If you live long you will harm the men ;
Because you are master, you can do now and then.
All things will be dear for the war,
Men of P—— Department trembling with tear.
All men with their families will cry for food,
Never expect that God will do you good.
Do not try to make reduction,
God will bless you for your action.
All say that Government service is best,
After fifteen years' service get rest ;
If we see uncertain is post of Government,
We will be excited to see the Russians that moment.
If you depend debit-checking upon postmaster,
You will get discredit and Government disaster.
If reduction is your chief intention,
Take the men who are entitled for the pension.
You are educated, rich, and free,
Don't touch whose service more than three.
You are being Christian,
Going to take away the bread of man."

It sometimes happens, however, that the native poet takes loyalty or love as his theme, and the result never fails to be amusing. The following lines on the occasion of the Duke of Connaught's first visit to India were submitted to an Anglo-Indian paper with a request for publication, and an intimation by the writer that "the beauty and style of the verses are of themselves my sufficient apology for troubling you to insert them in your paper " :—

"INDIA'S WELCOME TO THEIR ROYAL HIGHNESSES THE DUKE AND DUCHESS OF CONNAUGHT.

I.

Welcome ! Their Royal Highnesses the Duke and
    Duchess
Of Connaught, the Noble Prince and Princess
Welcome ! hail ! to thee thrice happy pair,
Such is the hearty joy, all Loyal subjects share.

II.

But India must be proud to sing in rhyme,
To see the Royal Princess for the first time,
And she cannot its full obligation express,
For confidence thus imposed by the Empress.

III.

Who will not long to see our Empress' third son,
As Major General of Meerut Division,
May his career be crowned with all success
Over the dales, Mountains and Fortress.

IV.

Oh ! it is in the hearts of the family Royal,
How the Natives of India are Loyal,
Especially the Parsees at the Prince of Wales' visit
    last,
What Loyalty they displayed, on such and many
    other occasions past.

V.

Lo ! there it is in sight the steamer's first sail,
So let us shout, congratulate, cheer and hail,
God bless the Empress and long may she reign,
Is the last chorus of the persons thronged in chain.

VI.

And as this verse's editor,
I remain, gentlemen and Dear Sir,
As Loyal subject and sincere,
Chinoy, Jehangir Ardeseer.

Bombay, 20th November, Eighteen Eighty-three,
Here is the conclusion and I am free." ·

Of love verses the following are fair specimens:—

"DEATH BY DISAPPOINTMENT IN LOVE.

I.

It is a pity that our city
    Should have lost so soon
A man so mighty, tone so witty,
    Sure a friend so boon.

II.

' 'Twas yesterday,' so people say,
    ' He went for walk at eve,
He went his way ; bright shone sun ray ;
    His heart with love did heave.

III.

' He walked as fast, till came at last
    To the garden close at hand ;
A glance he cast to seek repast,
    To have his mind's demand.

. IV.

' He saw just near his Beauty dear
 Below the Bamboo green,
She stood to hear th' addresses there
 Of him near her who'd been.

V.

' This man when he this scene did see
 With fury gnashed his teeth,
And said " O ! ye Gods ! shall this be ?
 Is he to win the wreath ?'

VI.

' " I so well prink, my clothes do drink
 Perfumes all fragrant fine ;
I give her trinkets nice ; to drink
 I give a precious wine.

VII.

' " And yet she goes to a man who knows
 Not what is gentleness !
Indeed she shows by her curved brows
 That him she loves. Oh, yes.

VIII.

' "Oh, yes, 'tis true."   So said he drew
   His kerchief o'er his eyes ;
His blood did brew ; he long did rue,
   And burst out into sighs.

IX.

' And now he had, to see that bad
   Scene, cast again his glare ;
He felt so sad, he went so mad,
   He gazed and gazed with care.

X.

' With eyes so keen he viewed the scene ;
   When clouds made matters worse.
The pair had seen the clouds, had been
   Now thinking to disperse.

XI.

' It now departs with wounded hearts
   With parting bliss of lips ;
The lover darts to kiss all parts
   And quick her bliss he sips.

XII.

' Our hero there, when his Love fair
   To part expressed her pain,
At heart did share the handsome pair
   In pain he did not feign.

XIII.

' Then him we found fall on the ground
   As if got mesmerized.
His eyes turned round ; he made a sound
   Which made us quite surprised.

XIV.

' Alas ! alas ! Now dead he was,
   Aground fell lifeless he,
His soul did pass, became his mass
   As cold as cold could be.' "

CHAPTER VII.

PETITIONS AND BEGGING LETTERS.

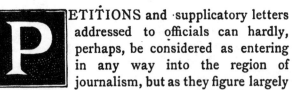

ETITIONS and supplicatory letters addressed to officials can hardly, perhaps, be considered as entering in any way into the region of journalism, but as they figure largely in the columns of the Indian Press a few examples may not be out of place. Before quoting them, however, a word or two by way of explanation is necessary. The production of petitions is quite an industry in India. Every town of any import-ance has its petition writer, as it has its solicitor or its doctor, and the larger towns have scores of the fraternity. They are usually men who have obtained a smattering of English education at one of the Government or missionary colleges, and who, having probably failed to obtain a position in the Government service, take to this work as a means of living; and a very lucrative career it sometimes is. The lower class Indian, whether he be a Government servant, or a domestic in the household of a European, has great faith in the efficacy of written appeals. It may be a rise of pay, a spell of holiday, or an appointment for some relative that he wants—whatever it is he avails himself of the epistolary talents of the petition writer, who for a modest sum speedily furnishes him with a moving appeal to his employer or official superior. There is no attempt made to conceal the source of origin of these productions. In the market places and street corners the ingenious scribe may be seen with his legs tucked under him, a rude writing pad on his knee, laboriously writing out, with the aid of a native reed pen about the thickness of a walking

stick, the communication which his humble patron,
who squats placidly by his side, pours into his
ear. Naturally in the process of translation the
sentiments of the customer are curiously presented, and as often as not the petition furnishes
material for merriment in the family circle of its
recipient. This, for instance, is how one petitioner prefers his claims to a certain appointment :—

"Respectfully Sheweth.—That your honour's servant is poor man in agricultural behaviour, and much
depends on season for the staff of life, therefore he
prays that you will favour upon him, and take him
into your saintly service, that he may have some permanently labour for the support of his soul and his
family ; wherefore he falls upon his family's bended-
knees, and implores to you of this merciful consideration to a damnable miserable, like your honour's
unfortunate petitioner. That your lordship's honour's
servant was too much poorly during the last rains and
was resuscitated by much medicines which made mag-
nificent excavations in the coffers of your honourable
servant, whose means are curcumcised by his large

family, consisting of five female women, and three masculine, the last of which are still taking milk from mother's chest, and are damnably noiseful through pulmonary catastrophe in their interior abdomen. Besides the above named, an additional birth is, through grace of God, very shortly occurring to my beloved wife of bosom. . . . That your honour's damnable servant was officiating in several capacities during past generations, but has become too much old for espousing hard labour in this time of his bodily life ; but was not drunkard, nor fornicator, nor thief, nor swindler, nor any of these kind, but was always pious, affectionate to his numerous family consisting of the aforesaid five female women, and three males, the last of whom are still milking the parental mother. That your generous honour's lordship's servant. was entreating to the Magistrate for employment in Municipality to remove filth, etc., but was not granted the petitioner. Therefore your generous lordship will give to me some easy work, in the —— Department, or something of this sort. For which act of kindness your noble lordship's poor servant will, as in duty bound, pray for your longevity and procreativeness. I have the honor to be, sir, your most obedient servant, ——, Candidate."

6

Here is another in much the same strain :—

" HONOURED AND MUCH RESPECTED SIR,—With due respect and humble submission, I beg to bring to your kind notice that for a long days, I have not the fortune to pay you a respect, or not to have your mental or daily welfare, therefore my request that you will be kind enough to show me some mercy and thankfulness, by pending some few lines to your wretched son and thereby highly oblige. In accordance by your verbal order, I am still lingering for your hopeful words, which I cannot put out from my memory or think not to be disappointed by you.

"Those words are not my fancyless imaginations, but a desire of ardent hope that I shall be patronize by you, and that patronizm and gratitude are ever remain in my heart from my eternity as long as I live in this world. Because I am out of employment more than a year, my mental faculties and conscience are daily swift away from my mind by which I shall afterwards jeopardize my future prospects, subject me to undergo many difficulties, and thereby makes me idle not to provide the necessary expenses of my family but to beg door to door.

" Cares and anorcities are the followers of my un-

fortunation to-days, by which I am as a pilethropic il-
(i. e. inner part is empty and outer part shows a very
good looking appearance.) Such is my condition.

"So my request to you that your sympathy and
philanthropic zeal will take some measure in my part,
by provide me a post either by you, or by your direct
patronage, to look with a favourable eye towards me
by showing some mercy and thankfulness.

"By the pray of the Almighty Father you have
placed in a high rank and you have the full capacity to
patronize a man like me, which I hope for a long time
not to be disappointed, but to remembered me as one
of your obedient servant give a sharp reply of this
wretched epistle and try for me the last, thereby highly
oblige."

There is such an amusing assumption of self-
satisfaction in the following that it also deserves
to be quoted :—

"MOST RESPECTFULLY SHOWETH,—That your petitioner being given to understand that your honor is
in want of hands to do the duties of signaller and
porters begs to offer himself as a candidate for one of
these : that your petitioner can read and write him

his own Vernacular and that he has a special gift of Almighty viz., he is a very tall young man beyond the ordinary hight of human population in this country where the inhabitants are mostly short, and that on this ground he will make himself more useful for the office of flag holder should your honor be pleased to confer me a situation I shall pray God for your long life and prosperity,

" Your most obedient servant,

"——.."

The following is a characteristic specimen of the native *takeed,* or reminder :—

" Sir,—As I am entertaining some skins of hope on account of the delay of my getting my certain reply.

" Is there anybody on the face of this earth who without any exertion through the path of study can have attained the true light of happiness ?

" It is not universally known that he, whose prospects is to cut a good figure in the world, must try his almost to burn insence in the temtle of study ?

" Why then, Sir, your honor, has put me in the godown (warehouse) to work through storm and lightening simply for four pice per hour ?

" Sir, your honor is throwing me from the highest pinnacle of hope to the lowest depth of despair !

" If your honor does not properly deem upon my regretful circumstances, then what shall I do ?

" If it did not lie within the compass of your honour's power, then I would have nothing to murmur. But if it is so, then I beg your pardon thousand times for so many botherations.

" I have the honour, &c.,

" ———."

Here is a sample of the poetical turn of mind which the petitioner sometimes displays :—

" Sir,—I respectfully beg to bring to your kind notice that I am still suffering much for my languishing life with a delusive hope of getting a job here at Bankurah.

" I have intended to enter in Police line for which I have already applied to the District Superintendent of Police hereof, but no .order as yet has been passed for the same.

"Thus being involved with a dark shadow of my glimping hope I am to pass my days pinning with ineffectual sorrows and endless anxieties.

"I have nothing but a barren hope to sustain my mind, I am still here at Bankurah crawling to get rid of the goal of my calamity by the blandishments of the Police Inspector and Revenue Police Sub-Inspector.

"I know not whether my good fortune is closed for ever or may be bloomed again. My lot, the spring of misery and sorrow has so much been prevalent that it has gained an everlasting ascendancy upon my good fortune and has monopolized its unrivalled occupation in me.

"Though I am deeply pressed and put into the deepest gulf of sorrow by my ill luck, my perserverence and fortitude must render me placid and hopeful to have been blessed again with your unequal love and favor. However my lot be cast, either to exalt me on high or cast me down headlong to the earth nothing shall efface the idea of your kind heart until death can put an end to my gratitude and hard life.

"Several importunities and expostulations had been referred to your honor by some previous letters, and to excite your love and keep it upright till to the last moment these mournful lines are drawn again. My next prayer shall carry the result of my application prodduced before the aforesaid Superintendent.

"My prayer has no object but to continue your love alike till to the moment when, by chance, my good fortune will be bloomed again by your love and favor.

"I am well hoping your honor to be the same.

"I have the honor," &c.

Of the domestic class of petition the following is a fair specimen :—

"GENTLEMAN,—I want to give trouble under your kind by these few lines, that the cook who is engaged some time ago under your kind favor, he is my married husband and he plays tricks with me, since he engaged in your favor. He never looks after me, neither he looks after my foodings, against all he puts me in debt for about expence, when he was sick and very near died, in that time, I borrowed money on interest and ate him.

"Respected Sir, what is my fault, that he is not agree in giving me food, and several times before he strikes me with a worse manner, and the same way he had done along with me, when I came yesterday under your kind favor to see him Parents, she came under your kind foot for getting my reward kindly justified in and make to me arrangements to let me give food and some for (Banga) from whom I borrowed money in his sickness for his medicine and for his eating. Or else you discharge him because since he engaged to you, he is too proud and never listen to me. By doing justice in my favor case, I shall ever pray for your long life and prosperity.—I am your most obedient slave,

"____."

Curious requests are sometimes preferred by natives to Europeans through the medium of petitions. This is how a native youth expresses the yearnings of his soul for a bicycle which a European stationed in a small up-country town was in the habit of riding :—

"Most respected Sir,—I fall at your feet ; if you please save my life and make me happy. I have the strongest desire to have the Biscyle to ride on.

Through the contemplation, I have no sleep either in
the day or in the night. I have been reduced to half,
and if I continue the same course, I do not know what
my fate will be. I have no money to buy it. Piety
has never become fruitless, and so the generosity.
Fame should remain after the man on the world, and
this is the duty which man should do. I have been
submitted myself to your honour, therefore your
honour should do whatever your honour likes. Your
honour should not think that you present me only a
Biscyle worth of sum rupees, but my life which will
perhaps serve your honour for your life. Now I have
become like a helpless sick person and you have become a doctor. If you give me medicine I shall
recover, otherwise not. Please be kind to me. God
will be pleased with you which is necessary for a man
to be happy. Let God excite tenderness in your
honour's heart. Let your great kind and noble mind
order your generous hands to present this miserable
man with your most beautiful ' Biscyle '—Sir, I am
your's most obediently," &c.

As a final example of this class of literature the
following plaintive protest against the burdens of
the Income Tax may be quoted :—

To His Excellency the Right Honourable Sir
Frederick Temple, Hamilton Temple, Black-
wood, Earl of Dufferin, K.P., G.C.B.,
G.G.M.C., P.C., F.R.S., D.C.L., G.M.S.I., Governor General of India in Council.

"Humbly showeth,—Pray hear our cry. If you
hear, the Almighty God will hear you. The small
portion of bread which we earn at the end of the day
by great toils is always found insufficient to appease
our hunger. Burning quarrel daily exists in our
family for more or less distribution of food. In the
face of these hardships the Government have extended
their hands towards our mouth and snatch a portion
of the morsel of bread. The Income tax collector says,
Government have assessed the income of Hindu undivided family. We are four brothers, four wives, and
six children, live together as undivided family. By
profession we are labourers. Our two brothers serve
as domestic servants on a monthly salary of Rs. 8 each,
and two wives as ayas on Rs. 5 each, other two
brothers are employed in the Public Works Department as labourers on a day wage of 5 annas each, and
the wives work in the same capacity on a day wage of
3 annas. A young-boy is a servant on a salary of
Rs. 2 8 4 per month. . . .

"The proportionate daily ration to each individual amounts very nearly to Rs. 3 14 3. We are required to maintain ourselves for a month within this sum. We are left without shoes and shows. We lead nothing but a miserable life. In the midst of these woes we see the mighty hands of Government recovers a portion before we receive our monthly earnings. We receive what we are paid with tears in our eyes and deep burning in our heart.

"Our neighbour—a widow and her brother's wife—are similarly oppressed. They cry in the same tone as we do. The income from their *Stri Dhun* (dowry) is assessed as an income of a Hindu undivided family. *Stri Dhun* solely belongs to the woman herself—is not recognized as a part of the family property, and no one can take it or its proceeds into family use. It is only for the women's maintenance after the death of those who survive them. Pray relieve *Stri Dhun* and income of persons in our position from the burden of the Income Tax. By doing this act God will give you long life and prosperity.

"Mark of Pandoo Deeta,
"Mark of Luxumon Deeta,
"Mark of Narayan Deeta,
"Mark of Krishna Deeta,
"of Poona."

CHAPTER VIII.

THE CONTENTS OF AN ANGLO-INDIAN EDITORIAL BOX.

EVERTING once more to matters more closely pertaining to newspaper work in India, our list of extracts may appropriately be closed with a few examples of the communications which find their way into the Editor's Box of an Anglo-Indian newspaper. They are taken at random from a heap of similar documents,

but they are fair types of their class, and will
afford some sort of idea of the many-sided character of the Indian journalist's correspondence.
First and foremost amongst an editor's contributors are the gentlemen who have the profoundest
admiration for his paper, but have the most
rooted objection to paying. for it. Many and
ingenious are the expedients resorted to to get on
to the Free List. That adopted by the writer of
the subjoined communication is, perhaps, the one
most commonly resorted to :—

"DEAR SIR,—It came to pass that once upon a time
I visited with your charming News the —— at one of
my friends, in devouring the contents of which I was
interested into more considerable bounds, whence I
was bent in the most high inclination to obtain it, but
no sooner it touched my heart than I felt myself
greatly discouraged at finding how my poor circumstance will allow me to pay the high subscription, but
eftsoons an idea of your generosity and kindness struck
to heart and incited me to bring to your kind notice by
means of a letter that with a kind enough value me as
one of your faithful correspondent, but I fear to gain

your compliance that probably you might set at naught me as I am a poor, but after all the idea of your noble and generous mind gives me solace and keeps me hopeful till you will not offer me your kind note. Strongly I hope that you will comply with my request being affected on my poor circumstance and the loss of half an anna, but I am in a great rue that my bad state disappoints you from subscription. I shall be very thankful to you, and ever pray to God to bestow His grace and kindness upon you and your family who esteems a man possessed of little or no fame for merit as I.

    "Yours true and faithful Parmeshar Dayal."

This is in much the same·strain :—

    "Most Honord and Litteral Sir,—I am poor man now taking trouble to write Your Honour. I am too much fond of mother tongue, alias English, and therefore being profoundly desirous to be master of this tongue, I am writing you. I am married man, my wife by the blessing of God has been too fruitful and thereby multiplying many sons and daughter, children causing severest distress to this poor petitioner's pockets in the pecuniary manner. But nevertheless I am strong minded and with energy and time will overthrow all the difficulties which do at present beset my matrimonial bed. As Sir, I cannot afford to purchase your universal renowned paper must asking of your Honour a great and magnanimous favour to letting me have free paper in order to magnify my intellect and in time become perhaps a author of some book or books may be. I will then remember your kind honour's great kindness and will ever circumcise myself to Your Honour your dutiful tutor and other things. I will write articles to your paper as payment can't give. I will make your Honour present of book when I write."

It will be observed that the writer of the above lays great stress on his desire to learn English, and promises contributions in return for the privilege he asks. This is a common method of baiting the hook which it is hoped will land the editorial fish, but it frequently happens that a correspondent offers his lucubrations not as a *quid pro quo* but solely in order that he may improve his English. Here is one such as is almost daily received :—

"SIR,—I am, as you already know, a Subscriber to your paper, ——. I see that news from these parts is very rare in your wide-spread paper.

"On the recommendation of a friend, I have thought of contributing to your paper a few lines every week ; *as a means of improving my writing* and doing at the same time some service to the public.

"Should you approve of it, the enclosed would be my first letter, which I beg you will kindly insert in your columns.

"I remain," &c.

Another correspondent writes :—

"SIR,—The accompanying packet contains a letter to be published in your paper. I am a perfect novice in writing in English. In fact this is the very first time that I write a letter in English. Several errors and even blunders as regards the rules of grammar, idiom, and the use of words might have crept in by reason of my ignorance, so I hope you will as a 'Tutor of the millions' correct every one of those mistakes and then hand it over to the compositor.

"I have come to you with hope which I am sure

you will not nip in the bud. Hoping that you will
not disappoint me,

"I am,

"Yours, &c.,

" A Moderate Indian Whig."

The Anglo-Indian is not only regarded as a
" Tutor to the millions," to use the expression of
the writer of the above, but he is looked upon as
the presiding genius of a sort of inquiry bureau to
be used by the public for the elucidation of the
most delicate problems. The following contributions speak for themselves :—

" SIR,—I have heard from a European gentleman
that he feels sick when he takes a warm foot bath. I
shall feel much obliged to know if any other gentleman
has got a similar experience.

"Yours faithfully,

"———."

" SIR,—I am suffering from that strange complaint
called by our Medical men Somnambulism, and have
consulted some of our best L. M. and S. [Licentiates of

7

Medicine and Surgery], and even of late tried to find relief from the quackery of native Hakims, but alas, all to no purpose. Having of late being troubled in an uncommon degree so as to become a source of endless nuisance to those around me, I make myself bold to ask your favour of finding me a short space in your widely circulated paper, and thus allow me to address myself to the elite of the Medical profession, or any of your numerous readers who would be good enough to suggest some effectual cure for that nasty malady. Of constitution naturally weak, I am hardly able to stand the severe strain of hard work which my daily calling entails,—all these conspire to tell considerably both on my physical and mental powers. Can drudgery of daily life and a weak constitution be the cause of Somnambulism ? which sometimes make me do strange and frolicsome tricks of which I am little proud. A timely advice for an effectual cure will be thankfully appreciated by

" OSTA."

" SIR,—Can you or any of your numerous legal readers be so good as to oblige a numerous family composed, for the greater part, of minors, by solving the following legal difficulty ?

"Is a Paterfamilias of 'Middle Station' justified to stint, or even semi-starve, himself and his numerous family composed, as said above, of minors solely dependant upon him?

"Cannot the Courts of Law bring their influence to bear upon such men, and bring them to their proper senses, and to mitigate the bitter distresses of young helpless children, worse off, under such circumstances, than orphans?

"LAW OF HUMANITY."

"SIR,—I would be highly obliged by your kindly admitting the following insertion in your valuable journal, and by the intelligible solution thereof graciously set forth in your column of world wide fame by some medical man your reader.

"What means should be adopted to remedy the ceasing of the substantial production of milk in a mother's breast, I am quite unaware of. Therefore anybody in *mercy to the Starving child*, by giving out some beneficial remedy would not only confer boon on the afflicting child but its patron too.

"Yours faithfully,
·"A POOR CHRISTIAN."

"SIR,—Will any of your numerous readers oblige

me by their answering the following questions : Where was the Garden of Eden situated? After Adam and Eve had sinned where did they live? Was Adam endowed with Animals language, and what kind of fruit they had eaten."

The above all indicate a generous confidence in the value of a newspaper as a medium for the solution of knotty problems. In the following letter, which is interesting also from other points of view, the writer seems to harbour the idea that the editor has power to act as well as to write :—

"SIR,—I hope you will have the pleasure to insert the following pathetic lines in your Paper and hope it will give some amusement to the Readers.

"A Man by name Heerajee, of Masen profession, has lately come to Hyderabad leaving his native land and property possessed with a strange notion, that is he is in a perplexity of mind to find a way for the remission of his sins; after all he has come to a final decision and dettermined this :—That on the Judgement day the Most Gracious Queen Empress of India and the Nizam of Hyderabad (My-booh-Alli-Basha) will appear before the Tribunal Judge Jesus Christ, and at the same time he will strive to get the water cleaned these boath Monarches feet and Jesus Christ will he drink and believes his sins are forgiven and he is in a ordend desire that this message would reach the ear of these Monarches for which purpose he is willing to exhaust all his money and time.

"Under these above stated events the Editor may consider over and extract his main object and issue necessary exertions so as to prevent him from his foolish idea.

"It appears his *guroo* [spiritual teacher] by name Thooka ram Sadoo has put this immagenary and strong idea into his brain.

"He is glad see this news published in any paper.

"Half anna Postege stamp herein enclosed for your early suggestion.

   "I beg to remain, Sir,

    "Your most obedient servant,

        "——.''

It also frequently happens that an attempt is made to air social questions of a delicate charac-ter in the columns of the Press. Here is an amusing complaint of the lack of good manners

displayed by a body of Parsees at one of their
caste dinners :—

"SIR,—I had gone to Poona for a business of mine
and I had stayed there for about two months, during
which time I had gone to each of the two Ghumbar
feasts. To my great sorrow I beg to bring to your
kind notice that I was greatly disgusted with the
behaviour of the invited there. All of the invited try
their best to secure seats for them to dinner as soon as
they can and in order to fulfil this desire of them, they
overlook manners and customs. Very serious cases
they do force to be occured! Some are tramped up
some are nearly crushed and the like. To my great
surprise I found in the second of the last Ghumbar
·feasts' which were given to Parsees in the 'Batleewala
Ageearee' a Bombay young man tramped up by several
foolish persons, a Parsee girl of ten heaped up by
almost a score and the like. Certainly this spectacle
to the eye of the wise is rude and totally disgustful.
Almost all of them were well dressed and looked like
gentlemen, but shame on their dress and person. Had
they followed what Dr. Goldsmith has said they would
have abstained from giving a trouble to a person like
me and the editor who has thought proper to manifest

their foolishness. Dr. Goldsmith has said, 'Handsome enough if they be good enough, for handsome is that handsome does.' The management was quite satisfactory and commendable but I humbly suggest the present managers of the Ghumbar feast to increase the dining room's space a little more which can be done with a little expense.

" ____ ."

Another class of contributions which finds full representation in the editorial box is anonymous communications making grave charges against Native States, officials, or private individuals. They are usually libellous, and more often than not malicious inventions or gross exaggerations. In the following quaint epistle which was submitted with the intimation that " I do not to inform you with my name, therefore I fearce from my life," there is probably from what one knows of the administration of Native States, a large amount of truth :—

" All the pains and dangers who are created in world by God, undoubtedly it is mading for resedences of ——.

"If any one tell to the public of —— 'that all cruels and pains wich was in former Kings reign peoples in this time are not it, and all men leave in security with glade' they do not trust of it ; therefore them goods and propertrys and lives are in hard danger and always they pasd him time in fearful.

"The fearce of them are onaccount the H. H. Nawab's cruel, because the H. H. is large userper and litte fault he punish very hard.

"Here is a prisoner *Anwarshuk Khan* he is about sixteen years in prison for custody of this prisoner is genral order, annualy he is binding in chain like those men who killding the men.

"Formerly he steals few things in one time of one person, but he is till in prison, and any one can not asked that what is cause of confine his in prison.

"Somany work hear are very many after this I will inform you.

"Good luck are those men that pasd you life in the English Government. Certainly ! Certainly ! ! Certainly ! ! !

"Yours obedient servant,

"TRUTH."

The same cannot be said for this communicated

paragraph which a " child-like and bland " native tried to palm off upon the unsophisticated European editor :—

" We hear that a certain partner in a respectably-mentioned local firm of native solicitors has been on briars and brambles for the past two weeks or three, owing to the threatened exposure of a certain colourable transaction he is deeply concerned in, and alleged to have been executed by him prior to enrollment. The transaction is said to relate to the insolvency of a well-known Parsee bankrupt, who benefitting extensively in the share-mania time came down with the critical crash ; and it is believed that this threatened exposure will, in all probability, bring in a good round sum of money into the pockets of his impoverished creditors. We are informed that the ignition is held in suspense until the views of a mutual friend over the sea are ascertained, who failing in bringing about a ' hush,' will be instrumental in delivering over the alleged culprit to justice to be dealt with in an exemplary manner."

Perhaps not unnaturally, the necessary suppression of effusions of the above and a like character creates discontent in the minds of the writers. Very often they give vent to their feelings in terms of mingled entreaty and anguish. One writer expresses sorrow to find that the editor did not publish a laboured and prolix biography of " one of his subscribers cut in the prime of life," and begs that in order " to comfort the deceased's family " the account may appear in a subsequent issue.   Another unburdens himself thus :—

" SIR,—I have already submitted for review a printed copy of some Urdu verses composed by me about 2 years ago when I was aged 15 years, but to my sorrow which attacks no such human knowledge to worth of notice, unless I see it is little patronized by a Lextrated man as yourself. I therefore most humbly beg to solicit the favour of your recommending the publice at your convinience, which will meet my just labour with the greatest thankfulness and ful of success.
                         " I have the honour to be,-&c.,
                                             "——."

A third correspondent is quite pathetic in his remonstrances with the stony-hearted editor :—

"Honoured Sir,—Judge of our feelings when we read that 'our letter could not be found room for.' In vain had we cherished the strong hopes that through you our grievances would be redressed. If you cannot publish the letter please be so kind as to publish its abridgment and let us know to the address below the faults you find with the letter. We have herewith sent to you postage stamps worth two annas to send the letter signed 'The Shackled' back to us. We wish to try our luck elsewhere, and if God destines us to suffer, it will awake no pity in any newspaper Editor. But to give us encouragement at so honourable an attempt let us know our faults and oblige. We must at the same time beseech you if the letter be very lengthy to give it any shape you please.

"Yours truly,

"——."

Here we must hold our hand. The list of curiosities might be indefinitely extended, but sufficient have been given to convey to the English reader some kind of idea of the amusing side of the Indian Press. That is an aspect of the subject which has hitherto received scant con-

sideration in this country.   Political matters have
monopolized all our attention, and we have only
been allowed to see the Indian Native newspaper
in the light of a disseminator of disloyal sentiments.   Probably this little work, if it does
nothing else, may help to dispel that illusion, and
show that while the indigenous Press of India is
crudely written, badly printed, and often a source
of merriment rather than instruction, it is not so
black as it has been painted.

UNWIN BROTHERS, PRINTERS, CHILWORTH AND LONDON.

THE ADVENTURE SERIES.

400 pp. each Volume. · Large Crown 8vo, Illustrated, cloth, price 5s. each.

1. **The Adventures of a Younger Son.** By E. J. TRELAWNY. With an Introduction by EDWARD GARNETT. Illustrated with several Portraits of Trelawny, Cuts illustrating his Greek Adventures, and an Autograph Letter.

2. **Robert Drury's Journal in Madagascar.** With Preface and Notes by Capt. S. P. OLIVER, author of "Madagascar." Illustrated with Maps and Curious Cuts.

3. **Memoirs of the Extraordinary Military Career of John Shipp.** With an Introduction by Major H. M. CHICHESTER. Illustrated.

4. **The Adventures of Thos. Pellow, of Penryn, Mariner** (Three-and-Twenty Years in Captivity among the Moors). Written by Himself; and edited, with an Introduction and Notes, by Dr. ROBERT BROWN. Illustrated from Contemporaneous Prints.

5. **The Buccaneers and Marooners of America:** being an account of the Famous Adventures and Daring Deeds of certain notorious Freebooters of the Spanish Main. Edited and Illustrated by HOWARD PYLE.

6. **The Log of a Jack Tar:** being Passages from the Adventurous Life of JAMES CHOYCE, Seaman. Edited from the Original Manuscript, by Commander V. LOVETT CAMERON. Illustrated.

" A library that can be sincerely welcomed."—*Globe.*

"The 'Adventure Series' has made a capital start."—*Speaker.*

" To lovers of adventure of the slashing and dashing order, we cannot well conceive of a more favourable selection for inaugurating what promises to be an entertaining series."—*Leeds Mercury.*

LONDON: T. FISHER UNWIN, PATERNOSTER SQUARE, E.C.

THE CAMEO SERIES.

Fcap. 8vo, half-bound, paper boards, with Frontispiece, price **3s. 6d.** *each.*

I.

THE LADY FROM THE SEA.

By HENRIK IBSEN.

Translated by ELEANOR MARX-AVELING.

"A powerful study."—*Notes and Queries.*

II.

A LONDON PLANE-TREE,

And Other Poems.

By AMY LEVY.

"True and tender poetry."—*Saturday Review.*

III.

WORDSWORTH'S GRAVE,

And Other Poems.

By WILLIAM WATSON.

"The choicely-worded, well-turned quatrains, which succeed each other like the strong, unbroken waves of a full tide."—Mr. COSMO MONKHOUSE in the *Academy.*

IV.

IPHIGENIA IN DELPHI.

With some Translations from the Greek.

By RICHARD GARNETT, LL.D.

"A very interesting and scholarly piece of work."—*Manchester Guardian.*

V.

MIREIO:

A Provençal Poem.

By FREDERIC MISTRAL.

Translated by HARRIET W. PRESTON. Illustrated by JOSEPH PENNELL.

"This charming poem. . . . The translation is very skilfully done."—*St James's Gazette.*

VI.

LYRICS.

Selected from the works of

A. MARY F. ROBINSON
(Mdme. Darmesteter).

Frontispiece.

"A dantier handful of tender fancies no reader of verse need desire."—*Glasgow Herald.*

SOME OPINIONS OF THE PRESS.

"The dainty 'Cameo Series.'"—*Pictorial World.*
"Exceedingly pretty."—*Saturday Review.*
"Mr. Fisher Unwin's charming 'Cameo Series.'"—*Woman's World.*
"Very prettily produced."—*Nonconformist.*
"Mr. Fisher Unwin's eccentrically-beautiful 'Cameo Series.'"—*Scottish Leader.*
"The 'Cameo Series' promises well. Is dainty in form."—*Star.*
"Will delight the heart of the bibliophile."—*Christian Leader.*
"Prettily bound and beautifully printed."—*Woman's Gazette.*

LONDON: T. FISHER UNWIN, PATERNOSTER SQUARE, E.C.

CPSIA information can be obtained
at www.ICGtesting.com
Printed in the USA
BVHW041026180719
553828BV00016B/1947/P